Fear

Fear
Psychological Study of the Causes and Effects

Charles Richet
James Sully

Man and Society Studies Collection

LM Publishers

Fear

I am afraid, oh I am so afraid!
The cold black fear is clutching me to-night
As long ago when they would take the light
And leave the little child who would have
prayed,
Frozen and sleepless at the thought of death.
My heart that beats too fast will rest too soon;
I shall not know if it be night or noon,—
Yet shall I struggle in the dark for breath?
Will no one fight the Terror for my sake,
The heavy darkness that no dawn will break?
How can they leave me in that dark alone,
Who loved the joy of light and warmth so much,
And thrilled so with the sense of sound and
touch,—
How can they shut me underneath a stone?

By Sara Teasdale

A Psychological Study of Fear[1]

Although the study of fear is very interesting, it has hardly yet been made in a methodical way. While some ingenious observations concerning it may be found in moral and psychological works, the physiologists and philosophers appear to have neglected this humble emotion.

The instructive work of the Italian, M. Mosso, gives an excellent physiological study of the physical phenomena of fear, but is almost the only treatise that bears on the subject. It is our purpose to look at it from the point of view of general psychology, and of

---

[1] By Charles Richet

9

the relations of man with animals; and to inquire into the effects and causes of fear among all beings capable of feeling it.

First of all, we have to describe the signs of fear and the physical phenomena that accompany it. With man, the testimony of his own consciousness is sufficient. With him fear may be wholly internal and translated by no apparent sign; but he can also afterward give account of his experiences. With animals the case is different. Their only language is their attitude. Our only resource for discovering the emotions by which they may be stirred is by the exterior signs they may give of them; and then we can only draw our conclusions by analogy. My horse all at once raises his head, droops his ears, shies, and starts on a gallop. There was a white cloth before him, and I conclude that he was afraid of it. Have I any right to draw such a conclusion? To affirm it with certainty in every particular, I would have - to use a vulgar expression - to be in his skin; for what I saw does not rigorously prove that my horse had a feeling identical with the one I am acquainted with from having suffered it myself, and which I call fear. Still, I have every reason for believing that the horse's feeling is of the same kind; for his attitude is the same when it thunders or when he hears a violent detonation, things which provoke fear in man; moreover, various other quadrupeds assume nearly the same attitudes when they are surprised by an unexpected object.

When we come to the lower animals it is extremely difficult to determine the operation of fear among them.

When frogs hastily leap into the water and swim for their holes at the passing of any animal along the edge of the marsh, is it fear that has moved them? Very likely, although their physiognomy has not changed - for they have none and we are not able to pass any judgment with regard to the phenomena of consciousness they may have experienced. We all agree that something has affected them that resembles fear in man.

Fear acts in two ways. At times it paralyzes and makes motionless; at other times it excites and gives extraordinary strength.

One person overcome by it remains fastened to the spot, pale and inert; his legs give way, and all his forces fail him. Another person scampers away like a rabbit. Fear gives him wings, and he abandons his unhappy companion, who is not able to move, while he has already put himself out of danger. At the same time special physical phenomena are manifested, which cannot be described better than in the language of the poets and the common people. The hair stands out on the head; the body is seized with trembling and with a general shiver, and the teeth chatter so that they can be heard. The hands shake so that they cannot grasp anything; the legs give way; a profuse, cold, clammy perspiration covers the body; the skin feels shivering, and the hair-bulbs over it swell up and harden. A convulsive thrill, with a feeling of cold, runs down the body, from the nape to the toe, coursing along the back at intervals like a cold electric wave.

The face grows pale, and the heart beats violently, as if it would burst out of the chest; or else, perhaps, it almost stops, producing a feeling of indescribable distress. The pupils dilate, the eyes open wide, and the features assume a repulsive aspect, which has been well represented by the great painters. The voice sticks in the throat, and the victim of the emotion is speechless. These are the manifestations of fear in one of its highest forms. They are less evident in moderate fear, according as it is moderate; while the most intense degree of emotion produces syncope, or arrest of the movements of the heart.

The syncope is rarely prolonged till death ensues; but well-authenticated cases are on record in which death has resulted immediately, while simple syncope is quite frequent. Most of the physical effects of fear, in fact, the pale face, the general weakness and paralysis, the buzzing in the ears, and the vertigos, are symptoms of syncope; and when they accompany sudden fright they are probably less due directly to the fright itself than to the arrest of the movements of the heart which it provokes. This profound emotion of fear, with its accompaniment of violent external phenomena, is fatal and involuntary, and is a reflex action, provoked by an irresistible force, independent of ourselves.

Besides the physical reflex actions, well known to physiologists and often described, I have defined a class of psychical reflex actions. Ordinary reflex actions, like the contraction and enlargement of the pupil under varying intensities of light, are dependent on the most simple excitations and require no intelligence, comprehension, or mental elaboration.

Other reflex actions are of a different character. They are reflex, in that they are involuntary; and conscious, in that we can give a complete account of them; but they are also psychical, in that a considerable degree of intelligence is required for them to occur. Take, for example, the simple instance of the soldier who dodges when he hears a bullet whistling near him. The motion is entirely reflex, for the poor fellow has dodged before he has even thought of the ball that might hit him; but it is also conscious and psychical. A number of analogous actions might be cited; and if we give the subject a little attention we shall find that they play an important part in our everyday life.

The conscious moral emotion and the exterior movement accompanying it are caused by a sensible excitation which in itself is nothing, but is transformed by the mind so as to become effective.

The whistling of a bullet as a mere noise would not cause one to dodge. It is a noise which, in itself, is quite incapable of provoking such a movement. If, then, the soldier dodges so abruptly, it is because the whistling of the bullet has a significance to him. He knows, without having thought long about it, that it is death passing by him. And before he has performed any conscious reasoning concerning the effects of a whistling bullet, the association of ideas has worked in his mind and determined his sudden movement.

If, while an athlete was performing his exercises on the trapeze, one of the cords should break, the host of spectators would be overcome by great emotion. Some of the women would turn away sick, and others would scream; and the bravest would shiver and turn pale. These phenomena are certainly involuntary and reflexive; but they could not exist without some intelligent comprehension of what has taken place. The breaking of a cord is not an excitant of reflex actions, and, if there were no man's life in the case, the crowd would not feel them.

The lower animals are not susceptible of having psychical reflex emotions, only simple ones; for they have no knowledge, and no judgment respecting the nature of the exciting cause. Many of man's reflex acts are of similar character, as the flow of tears, the reddening, and the vigorous winking when one gets a speck in his eye.

Nearly all the psychical reflex acts have as their starting point an excitation of the senses. Such excitations cannot of themselves be competent to provoke an organic reflex movement; but, if they are comprehended by an intelligence, and are accompanied by a notion of the exterior phenomenon, they can then determine a reflex act which is the consequence of that notion.

Thus, fear, as a psychical reflex emotion, results doubly: first, in a phenomenon of consciousness, or the fright felt by the *me*; and, secondly, in a series of characteristic reflex motive phenomena. The whole central nervous system is disturbed, and the disturbance is communicated to all the motive and glandular apparatus: to the heart, whose beatings are arrested or accelerated; to the muscles, which vibrate; to the salivary glands, which cease to produce saliva; to the intestines, which contract with force; to the vessels of the pallid face; to the sudoriferous glands; to the dilating pupil; and to the features, which reflect the distress of the consciousness.

M. Brown-Sequard has proved by numerous experiments that the nervous system, when it has been subjected to an exterior stimulation, may be excited or paralyzed. The emotions of fear are likewise either stimulating or paralyzing, or inhibitory. Examples of both kinds of effect are numerous. Thus, when a rabbit is overtaken by a dog, it runs away immediately, the faster the more it is frightened.

It will leap over wide ditches, pass through almost impenetrable hedges, and strike against objects it would ordinarily avoid, so much is its course precipitated by fear. If the dog pursues it, it leaps and bounds here and there, frightened out of its wits, but more agile and fleet in consequence of its very terror.

Another rabbit, under precisely similar circumstances of pursuit, instead of fleeing, remains still, for the sight of the dog's ardent eyes has inspired in it a fear of a character that will not permit it to withdraw its gaze. It is nearly paralyzed, and is incapable of running away, and fear, instead of making it run, prevents its running. Thus the same emotion is translated by an inhibition in one case, and by an excitation in another.

Very intense fear is generally inhibitory, or paralyzing in its effect, while a lighter fear works an increase of strength. It is known that anger develops muscular force to an extraordinary intensity. This is still more true of fear. A person who is running in fright will leap over obstacles which he would be wholly incapable of overcoming in his normal condition.

Numerous experiments show that the brain exercises an inhibitory action over the reflex movements, and that the more active that organ, the more they are under control. It is the will that exercises this power. Fear, likewise, may be modified and regulated, to a certain extent, by the will; and this is one of the most curious and mysterious phenomena in the history of the emotion.

We have said that psychical reflex emotions do not depend solely on the exterior excitation that disturbs the organism, but largely upon the elaboration of that excitation by the intelligence. The whistling of the bullet that makes the soldier dodge, the roaring of the lion which makes the dog tremble, the smell of the elephant which terrifies the horse, are in themselves indifferent excitations. They have power over the emotions only when they fall upon an intelligent organism which comprehends, with more or less of knowledge, what they mean. Hence the intensity of the fear does not depend upon the excitation itself, but upon the response of the organism to it. It depends upon our individual excitability, which is variable. Some men are naturally brave, others are naturally timid. Children are generally timid, women not so brave as men, and nervous persons less brave than phlegmatic ones. There are also bold and timid animals.

It is probably wrong to use, in distinguishing between individuals, the terms bravery and timidity. A nervous, timorous, and impressionable person may be extremely brave. He may, besides, be all the more deserving for that; but his temperament makes it easy to startle him; and it is hard to find a word to express his exact character. An extremely nervous woman may be capable of performing deeds of extraordinary bravery; but that does not prevent her suffering from fear. It is necessary, then, to distinguish between the emotion, of which we are not masters, and the acts which it commands.

There are two elements in fear: the sensational element or the emotion provoked in the consciousness; and the active element, or the series of acts which it induces. But in these acts it is necessary to distinguish between real actions performed by ourselves, and organic, visceral, and involuntary motions. The famous saying attributed to Turenne expresses a profound psychological truth bearing upon this point. When the battle had begun and the bullets and shot, rattling about him, made him tremble, he remarked to himself: "*You are trembling, carcass of mine; you would tremble more if you knew where I was going to take you!*"

In fact, the feeling of fear cannot be subdued. It is an irresistible emotion that depends upon our organization and one which all the most logical reasoning cannot change. Nothing is more true than the common saying that fear does not reason; and it is remarkable how little efficacy intelligence and its efforts have to arrest its effects. I know a highly intelligent person, with a strong and clear mind, who believes he would be lost if he had to go into a boat. Yet the sea is smooth, the course is short, and the boat stanch. Excellent reasoning, but it does not take hold of him.

His emotion is stronger than all the arguments you can invent, however irreproachable they may be, and no matter how fully the poltroon may recognize their force. How many children there are who do not dare to cross in the night the garden where they have played all day, where they know there is no danger, and where they will not lose sight of the lights in the house!

An instance out of my own experience will go to show how fear does not reason. About ten years ago, when I was in Baden, near the Black

Forest, I was in the habit of walking alone in the evening till late in the night. The security was absolute, and I knew very well that there was no danger; and, as long as I was in the open field or on the road, I felt nothing that resembled fear. But to go into the forest, where it was so dark that one could hardly see two steps ahead, was another thing.

I entered resolutely, and went in for some twenty paces; but, in spite of myself, the deeper I plunged into the darkness the more a fear gained possession of me which was quite incomprehensible. I tried in vain to overcome the unreasonable feeling, and I may have walked on in this way for about a quarter of an hour. But there was nothing pleasant about the walk, and I could not help feeling relieved when I saw the light of the sky through a gap in the trees, and it required a strong effort of the will to keep from pressing toward it. My fear was wholly without cause. I knew it, and yet I felt it as strongly as if it had been rational. Sometime after that adventure, I was traveling at night, alone with a guide in whom I had no confidence, in the mountains of Lebanon. The danger there was certainly much greater than around Baden, but I felt no fear.

The only effective means of obtaining the mastery over fear is by habit. It is with the moral emotions as with muscular exercise. To become a good walker one must be trained to it, by accustoming himself to greater and greater efforts every day till he arrives at the full extent of his powers. Habit has such an effect upon fear that nothing that is usual to us can make us afraid. Hence the frequency and ease of what is called professional courage. That kind of courage is not real courage; it is habit. The sailor on the tempest-driven ship; the doctor, the sister of charity, and the attendant in a pest or cholera hospital; the chemist and physiologist surrounded by infections, explosives, and poisons;

the aeronaut; the roofer, and the bull-fighter, do not exhibit the test of bravery. They are not afraid. The presentiment of an unknown danger, which is the foundation of all fear, does not exist for them. Operatives who work in factories of powder or dynamite are sometimes so imprudent and so little afraid of a danger which they are perfectly well acquainted with, but to which they are habituated, that it has become necessary to protect them against themselves, and to take rigorous measures to keep them from smoking and from using fire near the powder.

Real courage, as distinguished from professional courage, is the fearless confronting of a danger of which we recognize the importance and which we are not accustomed to.

Nothing is more variable than fear. It depends upon the individuality, or, rather, upon the excitability of each individual. Everyone has his peculiar quality of excitability, which depends upon his physiological and moral condition, and is not the same for the different excitations.

I believe that every man is more or less susceptible to fright; but that fear is caused among different persons by different motives. One is afraid of poisons, another of boats; one of bridges and mountains, another of snakes; another of darkness or of thunder; and each one can find among the excitations that strike upon his senses the one which will be most apt to provoke in him fear. The excitability of each person is also variable according to the time of day, or to his condition in health or disease. The thoughts do not follow the same course in a person who is hungry and in one who has just dined. A convalescent, debilitated by a protracted nervous affection, would doubtless be more accessible to fear than if he were robust, well, and just rising from the table. Attention and the imagination enormously augment the intensity of the emotion.

In fact, for all psychical reflex phenomena the excitement is nothing in itself; the reaction of the organism does all. The visual or auditory image which strikes our senses is nothing, so long as it is not transformed and elaborated by the intelligence in such a way as to become at last a frightful image. A child walking on the road at night sees a white cloth swinging in the air; he immediately imagines it a ghost in pursuit of him, and runs away terrified. His imagination has done it all, and if it had not amplified and immeasurably magnified the real image he would not have been afraid. Perhaps we ought all to be more modest than we have been in the habit of being respecting this matter of bravery, and to acknowledge that to be bold is often simply to lack imagination.

In some cases the imagination is blended with attention. To pay attention to an image is, by the fact itself, to aggrandize it and make it important, to give it relief, vividness, and force. Suppose one person should warn another that he is going to prick him with a pin at a particular point in the skin. For some minutes that pin-prick will have a menacing presence. All the force of the victim's attention will be borne upon it, though it is really inoffensive, and the thought will finally become almost painful.

If the same prick had surprised him without his having had time to think about it and concentrated attention upon the insignificant wound, it would probably have passed off unnoticed. But by virtue of attention it has become a great matter. So we may prepare for something we dread, and the long preparation will contribute to double our fear of it. Thus attention is, as well as imagination, an excitatory force, and may render extremely sensitive to fear persons who, without it, might have been bold to insolence. It is true that attention is voluntary to a certain point. We may, it is said, turn away our thoughts to some other subject. But attention can be commanded only when indifferent matters are in question.

Violent imaginings and strong emotions command it and are not commanded by it. Thus, from whatever side we regard the problem, we shall find that fear, whether as a sensation or as a conscious emotion, is dependent on our individual excitability and is quite independent of the will. Yet the will may intervene; but, however powerful we may suppose it to be, it has no effect on our feelings, but only on our acts.

The soldier who hears the bullets whistling around him cannot control his emotion, which is legitimate; but, by an effort of the will, he can keep from running away and continue to march on. Perhaps a still stronger effort of the will would be required to arrest the psychical reflex movement of dodging, but that is also possible. The will is, therefore, equivalent to a power of inhibition. The power is variable among different persons, and this variability occasions the different degrees of courage.

We have here, apparently, an antagonism between two contrary forces: on one side is the emotion, which incites to certain acts; on the other side is the will, or inhibitory power, which prevents those acts. It seems that when we are stirred by an emotion it can be best opposed by an inverse emotion.

The soldier in battle is sustained against his fear by the honor of the flag, the sense of personal dignity, the presence of his chiefs and comrades, ideas of duty and discipline, fear of chastisement, love of country, the hope of reward, and other strong motives. But the soldier's will and the factors that re-enforce it have no control over his organic movements. Though he can resist the inclination to run away and to dodge, he can not hinder himself from trembling and growing pale, or prevent the violent beatings of his heart and the cold sweat. It would therefore be unjust to reproach a person who has passed through a great danger for having become pallid and quaked. Turenne quaked, and he was not a coward.

There are, then, two kinds of bravery — that of the person who does not suffer from fear, which is easy and of little merit, and the bravery of a person who overcomes his fear. Such a person, in my opinion, is more courageous than any other; but, though I have great respect for him, I should put but little confidence in him, for his heroic effort may be overcome at any time, and virtue, beautiful as it is, is less solid than absence of emotion.

He who is overcome by fear and runs away with all his might is certainly not brave, and is not entitled to any eulogy; but we should be indulgent to him. Who knows whether, with a few words of encouragement or enthusiasm, or by becoming accustomed to danger, he might not have been able to conquer his innate sensibility? Doubtless the bravest also have their moments of failure; even if they have not yet had them, the time may come when, surprised by a violent, sudden, and irresistible emotion, they will not be strong enough to triumph over themselves.

We begin the inquiry into the function of fear in the animal economy with the assertion that none of the natural feelings are for nothing. Whatever theory of the origin of beings we adopt, we are always forced to recognize that everything within us serves some end.

Fear shows us where danger lies, creates aversion to that danger, and forces us to flee from it, and is, therefore, a protective instinct. We need to be protected.

If we had only our intelligence to inform us of danger, we should be very frequently in peril, and our existence would be greatly abbreviated. Nature seems to have a great distrust of intelligence, and to have given it an insignificant part in our self-protection. Emotion comes in first, and intelligence afterward. Wounds that make blood flow are dangerous to the organism; but, if we had to be convinced of the danger from this source to save ourselves from it, men would long ago have disappeared from the earth.

Nature has taken the simpler way of endowing us with such sensitiveness to pain that we avoid being wounded, not because the wound lets the blood flow, but for the more evident reason that it hurts us. So we avoid exposing ourselves to danger, not because it is danger, but because we are afraid.

Of the two elements in fear, the internal emotion, of which the consciousness takes cognizance, and the reflex action, all beings have the reflex element; but the emotion, so far as we can perceive, does not appear to be equally present in all.

Apparently, it is more powerful the more intelligence is developed; and inferior, unintelligent beings, feel neither pain nor fear with as much force as man. In passing from the brute to man, fear is transformed and generalized. With the animal it is instinctive, answering to no idea. The hen is afraid of the fox, without knowing that the fox may eat it; the gudgeon of the pike, without thinking of its voracity. The horse shies at the sound of thunder, without knowing that lightning can kill him. They are afraid without knowing why, perhaps even without knowing that they are afraid, while man, with his highly developed consciousness, has a perfect knowledge of his fear. Both man and the brute have in the same degree love of life, dislike of death, and fear in the face of danger. But the notion in the animal is so vague and indistinct that it hardly exists; it is translated by acts the significance of which escapes the actor himself, while in man the same idea becomes precise, reasoned out, and conscious.

What we call the instinct for self-preservation is only one of the forms of fear. A violent and irresistible emotion takes possession of our whole being when we perceive ourselves in the face of death, and is the manifestation of a love of life and dread of death that every man bears within himself. It requires real courage to do violence to this general and deep instinct.

We have, therefore, the following progression: The animal, by a simple reflex movement, reacts to excitations that threaten its life; and this reflex movement is admirably adapted to the necessities of its existence.

Next the reflex movement becomes more and more complicated, into a movement of the whole - with flight, outcry, and tremor.

Then, as the animal becomes more and more intelligent, emotion accompanies the action, till the animal not only responds to the menacing excitations by a movement of flight, but has also a conscious feeling of fear.

Finally, a superior degree of perfection appears in man. Besides the act and the emotion, intelligence is displayed, and the man comprehends why he is afraid.

The study of the reactions of the animal shows to what point all the instinctive movements provoked by fright are exactly conformed to the necessity of living, which Nature imposes upon each of her children. When a danger comes which it is necessary to escape, every animal has two means of deliverance. It can flee precipitately, or it can hide and keep still. I believe that the paralyzing and stupefying action of fear, which is manifested in man as well as in the animal, is a salutary instinct, which is probably transmitted from the animal to man, and which, if it is not useful to man, is evidently quite so to the animal. The reaction of immobility is so complete with some animals as to simulate death. There are various insects which, when they are touched, feign to be dead.

Every animal has its special kind of reaction. The butterfly flutters in capricious *détours;* the turtle withdraws into its shell; the bee, surprised by an enemy, stings him; the cuttle-fish empties its ink-bag; the hedgehog rolls himself up into a ball; other animals utter piercing cries. These are all reactions that represent different means of defense.

In studying the causes of fear, it is well to lay aside all rational and reasoned causes. When we know that our life is threatened, our fear is easily explained as the result of the knowledge. A man who is bound to the mouth of a cannon experiences a very strong fear; but, though legitimate, it is not a natural fear in the zoological sense of the word. He is in fear because he knows that his life is in danger; but this is a thought-out fear, reasoned and intelligent. Man's rational fears are the fear of death, the fear of pain, and the dread of disesteem. To the fear of death are ultimately referable all emotions of fear, whether conscious or not. Pain is a motive for dread even when it is not mortal, as, for example, in the case of a patient who is awaiting a surgical operation.

A more curious kind of rational fear is the fear of disesteem, which is felt by the orator about to make his address, or the actor of any kind to perform his part before the public. It can be assimilated, I think, to the dread that is felt by the patient about to undergo an operation, but is aggravated by the circumstance that, while the patient has only to be passive, the actor knows that the judgment of his audience will depend on himself.

In a milder form, it is timidity, such as is shown by young people still unused to society. We shall not enter into the psychological history of these moral fears, interesting as it might be. Nor shall we dwell upon the terror which is determined by the thought of danger and threatened death, for those feelings do not explain the origin of fear. Only the unthought fears can aid in that research.

There is a peculiar feeling, which does not seem identical with fear, though it is of the same character, which may be described as the vertigo of height. It is brought on by the view of a great depth. There is nothing rational in it, for there is no more danger of falling from a great height than from a slight elevation; and a slight barrier, even too slight to afford any real protection, is often sufficient to remove it. But it serves a protective purpose, in guarding us against the perils of elevated places. It is an excellent example of the psychical reflex affection, embodying all of its conditions of being involuntary, conscious, dependent on the sense of sight, and variable with different persons; and it is easily modifiable by education and habit.

The emotion excited by a sudden, violent noise is analogous to fear. It might be described simply as a rudiment of fear; a physical disturbance, or a visceral emotion, producing a momentary response in the mind. Many persons, for instance, are afraid of the sound of thunder. The noise of the storm tends to heighten the effect; and it is likewise observable in animals which, in tropical countries, show great distress during earthquakes and storms, and are also peculiarly sensitive to strident noises.

A loud noise, even when it is not unexpected, always causes a kind of surprise, which is manifested by winking and a general thrill, with palpitation of the heart. During the exposition of 1878 I watched the movements of parties of visitors who stopped to observe the operation of a pile-driver which thumped down every two or three minutes upon a post. The bystanders would shut their eyes at every crash of the machine, and I was not any more able than they were to keep from doing so.

Three other conditions favorable to the excitation of fear are those of the unknown, of darkness, and of solitude. The fear of the unknown has been named *misoneism, μῖσος, dislike; νέος, new*); or, to use a more familiar etymology, *neophobia.* It is best exemplified in children and savages; for in mature man use and reason have, as a rule, intervened to correct the instinctive feeling. An infant is nearly always afraid at the first sight of a strange animal, even though it be not very large, but may soon become accustomed to its presence. To savages also, whose intelligence is of an infantine grade, everything that does not enter into the line of daily objects is the subject of fear, when it is imposing in size and vigorous in movement, or of simple amazement when it is small and appears inoffensive. Higher minds, instead of shunning novelty, seek it eagerly. In the student, curiosity takes the place of neophobia. But that curiosity implies a degree of courage; for every unknown thing supposes a possible danger, and real complete security exists only in the face of objects the innocence of which we have tested. We are thus brought back by a rather tortuous way to what we have already said of habit, exercise, and professional courage.

Animals that are used to see man frequently cease to fear his presence. Domestic animals have no such fear of man as wild animals show. Animals also which have never been hunted show no fear when a person comes among them. The most cowardly animals are those which have been most actively pursued. The character of being wild and easily frightened seems to be one that is transmissible to descendants. Since there is no reason for fear existing when there is nothing threatening, the emotion in animals can be explained only by the fact that for series of generations they have been obliged to sustain themselves by flight against aggressors upon them. Neophobia, therefore, should be met among those animals which have experienced dangers, or whose ancestors have experienced dangers. It does not have to be shown that nearly all animals come under these conditions. The more unknown the unknown, the greater is the fear; and the fear of what are supposed to be supernatural phenomena is, where it exists, extremely great.

The effect of darkness in increasing or creating fear is explained by reference to the unknown as a principal cause of the emotion. Darkness is, in fact, the unknown. Light is the one of all the senses that tells us most clearly what is around us; and when it cannot perform its part we are of necessity unquiet and troubled. A man traveling in the open field in the full light of day sees everything around him, and goes on boldly in the knowledge that no enemy can escape his view. But if he is in a thick forest in the darkness of night, he imagines vaguely and without acknowledging it that the gravest of dangers may be awaiting him a step or two farther on. He may not think of particular dangers, but he is simply suffering from a causeless obscure fear that cannot be justified.

The darkness prevents him from seeing and distinguishing anything, and the mass of shade around him conceals the unknown, that is, possible danger or something frightful. Children and nervous women, being of a more excitable nature, are more sensitive to this influence than men, who are more able to check their emotions by reasoning. But I believe that no one can withdraw himself completely from it. This fear is also common to animals. All horsemen know that their horses are easily frightened during the night, especially when they are traveling on a road that is new to them.

Another condition, which contributes greatly to augment fear, is solitude. It is an abnormal condition. Man is before everything a social animal, and he cannot effectively protect himself unless he is sustained by some of his fellows. Hence that need of society under which a danger shared is confronted cheerfully and resolutely, while a danger to which one is exposed alone is often intolerable. This is the fact aside from the influence of self-respect and false shame, which, however, do not fail to play a part in the matter.

We frequently check the manifestations of fear so that no one may witness our cowardice. Perhaps none of us would be brave if we were not seen by anybody. On the word of all men who have encountered real dangers, solitary courage is the hardest and rarest.

Fear is augmented in solitude, by the thought that we are not protected by any one. Unless we have extreme confidence in ourselves, the feeling of helplessness under such circumstances becomes insupportable, and this without regard to whether our fear is justified or not. The company of anyone, even of an infant or an infirm person, is enough to reassure us. The most manifest sign of solitude is silence. A man must be really brave to resist the triple trial of the unknown, darkness, and solitude with silence. Let a familiar sound — the song of a bird, the striking of a clock, the noise of the sea or the wind, the rolling of a carriage, or a human voice - be heard in this solitude, and what a relief!

If we now look at the symptoms and causes of fear as a whole, we shall be able more clearly to understand the simple law that connects all the facts. All living beings are organized to live, and all their emotions and actions are conformable to this great purpose. Hence we have protective emotions or reflex phenomena, which cause us to flee from danger without intelligence and consciousness having to intervene, of which fear is one.

Man, whose intelligence can reach the causes and the laws of phenomena, knows that he must live, and the love of life is so solidly planted within him, that all that offend life - pain and death -

offer motives for fear. If a person is afraid, it is because the images of pain and death are before him.

Fear is, therefore, on final analysis, a protection against death. But salutary as it is, and inspired by nature, the feeling is one that must be energetically contended against, because it is an emotion of the lower class which it is necessary to try to dominate and make submissive to the moral conditions of our existence. We should try to conquer ourselves, and replace the notions of terror by the higher ideas which will perhaps triumph over fear, of self-forgetfulness, abnegation, duty.

These ideas will certainly not be without use; but a more effective means, perhaps, though a more humble one, is to habituate one's self to danger, and look in the face as often as possible, but without bravado and without anxiety, the figure of the death which awaits us all.

The study of fear (in Childhood)[2]

Fear is one of the characteristic feelings of the child. It seems to belong to these weakly things, brought face to face with a new, strange world, to tremble. They are naturally timid, as all that is weak and ignorant in Nature is apt to be timid.

I have said that fear is well marked in the child. Yet, though it is true that fully developed fear or terror shows itself by unmistakable signs, there are many cases where it is difficult to say whether the child is the subject of fear. Thus the reflex movement of a start on

---

[2] By James Sully in *Studies of Childhood.*

hearing a sound does not amount to fear, though it is akin to fear. Again, a child may show a sort of aesthetic dislike for an ugly form or sound, turning away in evident aversion, and yet not be afraid in the full sense. Fear proper betrays itself in the stare, the grave look, and in such movements as turning away and hiding the face against the nurse's or mother's shoulder. In severer forms it leads to trembling and to wild shrieking. Changes of color also occur. It is commonly said that great fear produces paleness; but, according to one of my correspondents, a child may show fear by his face turning scarlet. Fear, if not very intense, leads to voluntary movements — as turning away, putting the object away, or going away. In its more violent forms, however, it paralyzes the child. It is desirable that parents should carefully observe and describe the first signs of fear in their children.

It may be well to begin our study of fear by a reference to startling effects. As is well known, sudden and loud sounds, as that of a door banging, will give a shock to an infant in the first weeks of life, which, though not amounting to fear, is its progenitor. A clearer manifestation occurs when a new and unfamiliar sound calls forth the grave look, the trembling lip, and possibly the fit of crying. Darwin gives an excellent example of this. He had, he tells us, been accustomed to make all sorts of sudden noises with his boy, aged four months and a half, which were well received; but one day, having introduced a new sound—that of a loud snoring—he found that the child was quite upset, bursting out into a fit of crying.

As this incident suggests, it is not every new sound which is thus disconcerting to the little stranger. Sudden sharp sounds seem to be especially disliked, as those of a dog's bark. Loud and voluminous sounds, too, have a terrifying effect. The big noise of a factory, of a steamship, of a passing train, are among the causes alleged by my correspondents of this early startling and terrifying effect. My little girl when taken into the country at the age of nine months, though she liked the animals she saw on the whole, showed signs of fear on hearing the bleating of the sheep, by seeking shelter against the nurse's shoulder. So strong is this effect of suddenness and volume of sound that even musical sounds often excite some alarm at first. "He (a boy of four months) cried when he first heard the piano," writes one lady, and this is but a sample of many observations. A child of five months and a half showed such a horror of a banjo that it would scream if it were played or only touched. Preyer's boy, at sixteen months, was apparently alarmed when his father, in order to entertain him, produced a pure musical tone by rubbing a drinking-glass. He remarks that this same sound had been produced when the child was four months old without any ill effects.

This last fact suggests that such shrinkings from sound may be developed at a comparatively late date. This idea is supported by other observations. "From about two years four months (writes a mother) to the present time (two years and eleven months) he has shown signs of fear of music. At two years five months he liked some singing of rounds, but when a fresh person with a stronger voice than the rest joined, he begged the singer to stop. Presently he tolerated the singing as long as he might stand at the farthest corner of the room." This child was also about the same time afraid of the piano, and of the organ, when played by his mother in a church.

It is sometimes supposed that this startling effect of loud sounds is wholly an affair of nervous disturbance. But the late development of the repugnance in certain cases seems to show that this is not the only cause at work. Of course, a child's nervous organization may, through ill health, become more sensitive to this disturbing effect. But I suspect that vague alarm at the unexpected and unknown takes part here. There is something uncanny to the child in the very production of sound from a usually silent thing. A banjo lying now inert, harmless, and then suddenly firing out a whole gamut of sound may well shock a small child's preconceptions of things. The second time that fear was observed in our child at the age of ten months it was excited by a new toy which squeaked on being pressed. This seems to be another example of the disconcerting effect of the unexpected. In other cases the alarming effect of the mystery is increased by the absence of all visible cause. One little boy of two years used to get sadly frightened at the sound of the water rushing into the cistern which was near his nursery. The child was afraid at the same time of thunder, calling it "water coming."

I am far from saying that all children manifest this fear of sounds-Miss Shinn points out that her niece was from the first pleased with the piano, and this is no doubt true of many children. Children behave very differently toward thunder, some being greatly disturbed by it, others being rather delighted. Thus Preyer's boy, who was so ignominiously upset by the tone of the drinking-glass, laughed at the thunderstorm; and we know that the little Walter Scott was once found during a thunderstorm lying on his back in the open air clapping his hands and shouting "Bonnie, bonnie!" at the flashes of lightning. It is possible that in such cases the exhilarating effect of the brightness counteracts the uncanny effect of the thunder. More observations are needed on this point.

A complete explanation of these early vague alarms of the ear may as yet not be possible. Children show in the matter of sound capricious repugnances which it is exceedingly difficult to account for. They seem sometimes to have their pet aversions like older folk.

But I think a general explanation is possible.

To begin with, then, it is probable that in many of these cases, especially those occurring in the first six months, we have to do with an organic phenomenon, with a sort of jar to the nervous system. To understand this we have to remember that the ear is, in the case of man at least, the sense-organ through which the nervous system is most powerfully and profoundly acted on. Sounds seem to go through us, to pierce us, to shake us, to pound and crush us. A child of four or six months has a nervous organization still weak and unstable, and we should naturally expect loud sounds to produce a disturbing effect on it.

To this it is to be added that sounds have a way of taking us by surprise, of seeming to start out of nothing; and this aspect of them, as I have pointed out above, may well excite vague alarm in the small creatures to whom all that is new and exceptional is apt to seem uncanny. The fact that most children soon lose their fear by getting used to the sounds seems to show how much the new and the mysterious has to do with the effect.

Whether heredity plays any part here in the fear of the dog's barking and other sounds of animals seems to me exceedingly doubtful. This point will, however, come up for closer consideration presently, when we deal with children's fear of animals.

Before considering the manifold outgoings of fear produced by impressions of the eye, we may glance at another form of early disturbance which has some analogy with the shocklike effects of certain sounds. I refer here to the feeling of bodily insecurity which appears very early when the child is awkwardly carried, or let down back foremost, and later when it begins to walk. One child in her fifth month was observed, when carried, to hold on to the nurse's dress as if for safety. And it has been noticed by more than one observer that on dandling a baby up and down on one's arms, it will on descending—that is, when the support of the arms is being withdrawn—show signs of discontent in struggling movements.

Bell, Preyer, and others regard this as an instinctive form of fear. Such manifestations may, however, be merely the result of sudden and rude disturbances of the sense of bodily ease which attends the habitual condition of adequate support. A child accustomed to lie in a cradle, on the floor, or in somebody's lap, might be expected to be put out when the supporting mass is greatly reduced, as in bad carrying, or wholly removed, as in quickly lowering the child backward. The fear of falling, which shows itself on the child's first attempting to stand, comes, it must he remembered, as an accompaniment of a new and highly strange situation. The first experience of using the legs for support must, one supposes, involve a profound change in the child's whole bodily consciousness—a change which may well be accompanied with a sense of disturbance. Not only so, it comes after a considerable experience of partial failings, as in trying to turn over when lying, half climbing the sides of the cradle, etc., and still ruder bumpings when the crawling stage is reached. These would, I suspect, be quite sufficient to produce the timidity which is observable on making the bolder venture of standing.

Fears excited by visual impressions come later than those excited by sounds. The reason of this seems pretty obvious. Visual sensations do not produce the strong effect of nervous shock which auditory ones produce. Let a person compare the violent and profound jar which he experiences on suddenly hearing a loud sound with the slight surface agitation produced by a sudden movement of an object across the field of vision. The latter has less of the effect of nervous jar and more of the characteristics of fear proper — that is, vague apprehension of evil. We should accordingly expect that eye-fears would only begin to show themselves in the child after experience had begun its educative work.

At the outset it is well, as in the case of ear-fear, to keep before us the distinction between mere dislike to a sensation and a true reaction of fear. We shall find that children's quasi-aesthetic dislikes to certain colors may readily simulate the appearance of fears.

Among the earliest manifestations of fear excited by visual impressions we have those called forth by the presentation of something new and strange, especially when it involves a rupture of customary arrangement. Although children love and delight in what is new, their disposition to fear is apt to give to new and strange objects a disquieting if not distinctly alarming character. This apprehension shows itself as soon as the child has begun to be used or accustomed to a particular state of things.

Among the more disconcerting effects of the ruder departure from the customary we have that of change of place. At first the infant betrays no sign of disturbance on being carried into a new room. But when once it has grown accustomed to certain rooms it will feel a new room to be strange, and eye its features with a perceptibly anxious look. My little girl at the age of seven months and a third gave unmistakable signs of such vague apprehension on changing her abode — a change which involved that of human surroundings also. She looked about her half wonderingly, half timidly, struck by the strangeness of the scenery, of the faces, and of the voices. Later, when experience and imagination are added, a child will show a still more marked shrinking from strange rooms. Thus a boy retained up to the age of three years and eight months the fear of being left alone in strange hotels or lodgings. Yet entrance on a strange abode does not by any means always excite this reaction.

A child may have his curiosity excited, or may be amused by the odd look of things. Thus one boy, on being taken at the age of fifteen months to a fresh house and given a small plain room, looked round and laughed at the odd carpet. Children even of the same age appear in such circumstances to vary greatly with respect to the relative strength of the impulses of fear and curiosity.

How different children's mental attitude may be toward the new and unfamiliar is illustrated by some notes on a boy sent me by his mother. This child, "though hardly ever afraid of strange people or places, was very much frightened as a baby of *familiar things seen after an interval.*" Thus "at ten months he was excessively frightened on returning to his nursery after a month's absence. On this occasion he screamed violently if his nurse left his side for a moment for some hours after he got home, whereas he had not in the least objected to being installed in a strange nursery." The mother adds that "at thirteen months, his memory having grown stronger, he was very much pleased at coming to his home after being away a fortnight." This case looks puzzling enough at first and seems to contradict the laws of infant psychology. Perhaps the child's partial recognition was accompanied by a sense of the uncanny, like that which we experience when a place seems familiar to us, though we have no clear recollection of having seen it before.

What applies to places applies also to persons; a sudden change of customary human surroundings by the arrival of a stranger on the scene is apt to trouble the child.

At first all faces seem alike to the child. Later, unfamiliar faces excite something like a grave inquisitorial scrutiny. Yet for the first three months there is no distinct manifestation of fear of strangers. It is only later, when attachment to human belongings has been developed, that the intrusion of strangers, and especially the proposal of a stranger to take the child, calls forth clear signs of displeasure and the shrinking away of fear.

Preyer gives the sixth and seventh month as the date at which his boy began to cry at the sight of a strange face. In one set of notes sent me it was remarked that a child four months and a half old would cry on being nursed by a stranger.

To be nursed by a stranger, however, is to have the whole baby world revolutionized: little wonder, then, that it should bring the feeling of strangeness and homelessness (*unheimlichkeit*).

Here, too, curious differences soon begin to disclose themselves, some children being decidedly more sociable toward strangers than others. It would be curious to compare the age at which children begin to take kindly to strangers. Preyer gives nineteen months as the date at which his boy surmounted his timidity; but it is probable that the transition occurs at very different dates in the case of different children.

I should like to add that the little boy to whom I referred just now displayed the same signs of uneasiness at seeing old friends after an interval, as at returning to old scenes. When eight months old "he moaned in a curious way when his nurse (of whom he was very fond) came home after a fortnight's holiday." Here, however, the signs of fear seem to be less pronounced than in the case of returning to the old room. It would be difficult to give the right name to this curious moan.

Partial alteration of the surroundings frequently brings about a measure of this same mental uneasiness. C…'s disturbance at the age of twelve weeks at finding his mother in a new dress is paralleled by the apprehensions of Preyer's boy when one year and five months old on seeing his mother in a black dress.

The second observation, read in the light of the first, seems to suggest that a change from the customary rather than anything appalling looking in the black color itself was here the source of the boy's trouble. This is borne out by another observation sent me. A child manifested between the ages of six or eight months and two years and a half the most marked repugnance to new clothes, so that the authorities found it very difficult to get them on. It is presumable that the donning of new apparel disturbed too rudely the child's sense of his proper self, and begot an uncanny feeling of another put in place of the old familiar child.

In certain cases the introduction of new natural objects of great extent and impressiveness will produce a similar effect of childish anxiety, as though they made too violent a change in the surroundings. One of the best illustrations of this obtainable from the life of an average well-to-do child is the impression produced by a first visit to the sea. Preyer's boy, at the age of twenty-one months, showed all the signs of fear when his nurse carried him on her arm close to the sea.

The boy C..., on being first taken near the sea at the age of two, was disturbed by its noise. While, however, I have a number of well-authenticated cases of such an instinctive repugnance to and something like dread of the sea, I find that there is by no means uniformity in children's behavior in this particular. A little boy who first saw the sea at the age of thirteen months, exhibited signs not of fear but of wondering delight, prettily stretching out his tiny hands toward it as if wanting to go to it. Another child, who also first saw the sea at the age of thirteen months, began to crawl toward the waves. And yet another boy at the age of twenty-one months, on first seeing the sea, spread his arms as if to embrace it.

These observations show that the strange big thing affects children very differently. C... had a particular dislike to noises, which was, I think, early strengthened by finding out that his father had the same prejudice. Hence, perhaps, his hostile attitude toward the sea.

Probably, too, imaginative children, whose minds take in something of the bigness of the sea, will be more disposed to this variety of fear. A mother writes me that her elder child, an imaginative girl, has not, even now at the age of six, got over her fear of going into the sea; whereas her sister, fifteen months younger and not of an imaginative temperament, is perfectly fearless. She adds that it is the bigness of the sea which evidently impresses the imagination of the elder.

Imaginative children, too, are apt to give life and purpose to the big, moving, noisy thing. This is illustrated in M. Pierre Loti's graphic account of his first childish impressions of the sea, seen one evening in the twilight. "It was of a dark, almost black-green; it seemed restless, treacherous, ready to swallow; it was stirring and swaying everywhere at the same time, with the look of sinister wickedness.

There seems enough in the vast waste of unresting waters to excite the imagination of a child to awe and terror.

Hence it is needless to follow M. Loti in his speculations as to an inherited fear of the sea. He seems to base this supposition on the fact that at this first view he distinctly recognized the sea. But such recognition may have meant merely the objective realization of what had, no doubt, been before pretty fully described by his mother and aunt, and imaginatively pictured by himself.

The opposite attitude — that of the thoroughly unimaginative child — in presence of the sea is well illustrated by the story of the little girl, aged two, who, on being first taken to see the watery wonder, exclaimed, "mamma, look at the soapy water!" The awful mystery of all the stretch of ever-moving water was invisible to the child, being hidden behind the familiar detail of the "soapy" edge.

There is probably nothing in the natural world which makes on the childish imagination quite so awful an impression as the watery leviathan. Perhaps the fear which one of my correspondents tells me was excited in her when a child by the sudden appearance of a mountain may be akin to this dread of the sea.

We may now pass to another group of fear-excitants — the appearance of certain strange forms and movements of objects.

The close connection between æsthetic dislike and fear is seen in the well-marked recoil of a child of thirteen months at the sight of an ugly doll. The said doll is described as a black doll with woolly head, startled eyes, and red lips. Such an ogre of a doll might well call up a tremor in the bravest of children.

In another case, that of a little boy of two years and two months, the broken face of a doll proved to be highly disconcerting. The mother describes the effect as a mixture of fear, distress, and intellectual wonder. Nor did his anxiety depart when, some hours later, the doll, after sleeping in his mother's room, reappeared with a new face.

In such cases, it seems plain, it is the ugly transformation of something familiar and agreeable which excites the feeling of nervous apprehension. Making grimaces—that is, the spoiling of the typical familiar face—may disturb a child even at the early age of two months. Such transformations are, moreover, not only ugly but bewildering, and where all is mysterious and uncanny the child is apt to fear.

Children, like animals, will sometimes show fear at the sight of what seem to us quite harmless objects. A shying horse is a puzzle to his rider, his terrors are so unpredictable. Similarly in the case of a timid child, almost anything unfamiliar and out of the way, whether in the color, the form, or the movement of an object, may provoke a measure of anxiety. Thus a little girl aged one year and ten months showed during a drive signs of fear at a row of gray ash trees placed along the road. This was just the kind of thing that a horse might be expected to shy at.

As with animals, so with children, any seemingly uncaused movement is apt to excite a feeling of alarm. Just as a dog will run away from a leaf whirled about by the wind, so children are apt to be terrified by the strange and quite irregular behavior of a feather as it glides along the floor or lifts itself into the air.

In these cases we may suppose that we have to do with a germ of superstitious fear which seems commonly to have its starting point in the appearance of something exceptional and uncanny that is unintelligible, and so smacking of the supernatural. The fear of feathers as uncanny objects plays, I am told, a considerable part in the superstitions of folklore. Such apparently selfcaused movement, so suggestive of life, might easily give rise to a vague sense of a mysterious presence or power possessing the object, and so lead to a crude form of a belief in supernatural agents.

In other cases of unexpected and mysterious movement the fear is slightly different. A little boy, when a year and eleven months, was frightened when visiting a lady's house by a toy elephant which shook its head. The same child, writes his mother, "at one year and seven months was very much scared by a toy cow which mooed realistically when its head was moved. This cow was subsequently given to him at about two years and three months. He was then still afraid of it, but became reconciled soon after, first allowing others to make it moo if he was at a safe distance, and at last making it moo himself."

There may possibly have been a germ of the fear of animals here; but I suspect that it was mainly a fear of the signs of life (movement and sound) appearing when they are not expected and have an uncanny aspect. The close simulation of a living thing by what is known to be not alive is disturbing to the child as to the adult. He will make his toys alive by his own fancy, but resent their taking on the full semblance of reality. In this sense he is a born idealist and not a realist. More careful observations on this curious group of child-fears are to be desired.

www.ingramcontent.com/pod-product-compliance
Lightning Source LLC
Chambersburg PA
CBHW022122280326
41933CB00007B/500